THE CELTS OF

NORTHERN EUROPE

*W*ith special thanks to Professor Catherine McKenna, Coordinator of the Medieval Studies Program at the Graduate School of the City University of New York and President of the Celtic Studies Association of North America.

CULTURES
OF THE PAST

THE
CELTS OF
NORTHERN EUROPE

KATHRYN HINDS

BENCHMARK BOOKS

MARSHALL CAVENDISH
NEW YORK

To Arthur and Owen

With thanks to Mom and Dad, Jane and Dudley, Stasia and Paul, and my editor, Joyce Stanton. You all helped make this book happen, and I couldn't have done it without you.

Benchmark Books
Marshall Cavendish Corporation
99 White Plains Road
Tarrytown, New York 10591-9001

© Marshall Cavendish Corporation 1997

Library of Congress Cataloging-in-Publication Data

Hinds, Kathryn, date.
   The Celts of northern Europe / by Kathryn Hinds.
      p.   cm. — (Cultures of the past)
   Includes bibliographical references and index.
   ISBN 0-7614-0092-3 (lib. bdg.)
   1. Celts—Juvenile literature.   I. Title.   II. Series.
D70.H56   1997
948'.004916—dc20   95-44101

SUMMARY: Introduces the tribes, customs, deities, and ideals of the Celtic people; reveals their contribution to the arts; discusses important events, people, and the legacy of the early Celts; and provides a chronology.

Printed in Hong Kong

Book design by Carol Matsuyama
Photo research by Barbara Scott

Front cover: A man wearing a horn helmet grasps a wheel in a scene from the Gundestrup Cauldron, found in a Danish peat bog in 1891.
Back cover: A reconstruction of the entrance to a Celtic temple in southern France

CONTENTS

CHAPTER ONE

TRIBES ON THE MOVE

In central Europe about 2,700 years ago, a remarkable people arose. Aggressive, proud, exuberant, and freedom loving, their many tribes shared common languages, political and social structures, economic systems, religious ideas, and artistic styles. They were called the Celts (kelts), and their distinctive culture eventually reached almost every part of Europe, with a legacy that lives on to the present day.

This bronze mask from one of the earliest known Celtic settlements expresses the sense of mystery that so often surrounds the history and beliefs of the ancient Celts.

Salt and Iron

One of the earliest centers of Celtic power was a place called Hallstatt (HALL-shtaht) in what is now Austria. At Hallstatt there was a huge deposit of salt, which the people had been mining and exporting over a wide area for centuries. Salt was extremely important for preserving food in ancient times, so Hallstatt became very wealthy. The community was also located near major trade routes. This fact not only helped the salt business but also brought the Hallstatt Celts into contact with many other cultures, such as those from around the Mediterranean, Baltic, and Black Seas.

By around 700 B.C.E.,* the people of the Hallstatt region had begun to make weapons and tools out of iron instead of bronze. This change in technology had far-reaching effects. Iron was much harder and more durable than bronze, and it kept a sharper edge.

*Many systems of dating have been used by different cultures throughout history. This series of books uses B.C.E. (Before Common Era) and C.E. (Common Era) instead of B.C. (Before Christ) and A.D. (Anno Domini) out of respect for the diversity of the world's peoples.

From their beginnings the Celts were gifted metalworkers. This miniature bronze cart, fourteen inches (thirty-five centimeters) long, may have symbolized the soul's journey to the otherworld, or afterlife. It was buried inside a mound along with the ashes of a Celtic ruler.

Celtic migration reached its northernmost extent in the Orkney Islands, just north of the Scottish mainland. The Celts who settled in the Orkneys and northern Scotland were called Picts. Very little about them is known, but the remains of many of their villages can still be seen.

With plowshares made of iron, the Celts could farm heavier, more fertile soils. Cattle could be raised more efficiently, too, because with iron scythes hay could be easily cut to store for winter feed. And iron made superior weapons.

Armed with iron swords and spearheads, the Celts streamed out of their homeland in search of fresh grazing and farmland. Warriors fought their way into new territory, followed by their

families, herds, and cartloads of possessions. The Hallstatt culture spread rapidly across Europe, covering what is now northern France, Belgium, southern Germany, Switzerland, Austria, the Czech Republic, Slovakia, and Hungary. By about 600 B.C.E. Celts were settled in northeast Scotland, and it may have been soon afterward that they reached Ireland.

By 450 B.C.E. the center of Celtic power had shifted from central Europe to western Europe, and a new era of Celtic culture was beginning. It is called La Tène (lah TEHN), after a place in Switzerland where archaeologists found large amounts of Celtic metalwork produced in a distinctive new style.

There were now many Celtic tribes. They seem to have been constantly fighting one another and constantly on the move in search of fresh lands. There were new migrations into regions that already had Celtic populations, such as Ireland. In addition the Celts established themselves in even more areas of Europe than before, including Britain, northwestern Spain, southern France—and northern Italy, where they made their greatest enemies.

From Germany, an early example of the La Tène art style. This gold-and-bronze cover was made to fit over a wooden bowl.

Rome's Celtic Nightmare

In about 400 B.C.E., with no warning, several Celtic tribes poured over the Alps to invade Etruscan territory in northern Italy. There they settled in simple farming villages. Before long, many of these Celts began to move south again in search of more land. This quest was bound to bring them into conflict with the Romans, who were steadily enlarging their own territory and influence.

9

CHARIOT WARFARE

The La Tène–era Celts had a powerful new weapon: the two-wheeled, iron-tired war chariot. It made them fearsome enemies as they thundered through Europe.

Celtic war chariots were lightweight, usually made of wicker but sometimes having wooden sides. The chariots were pulled by two small horses, which wore harnesses and trappings that were often decorated with elaborate metalwork. The chariots, too, had ornate metal fittings. A Roman historian even described a silver-plated Celtic chariot.

A chariot carried a charioteer and a warrior. These two people were often close friends. (In one Irish tale a king's charioteer is his sister.) The charioteer drove the vehicle wildly across the battlefield while the warrior cast his spears into the enemy ranks. Then the warrior jumped out of the chariot to fight with his sword. The charioteer backed off—but often stayed close enough to urge the warrior on—and then picked up the warrior again when necessary.

Chariot warriors were extraordinarily skillful and performed many daring feats. Some were known to balance themselves on the pole to which the horses were harnessed—while the chariot was moving at top speed. According to one early Irish tale, the warriors practiced such feats by doing acrobatics on ropes stretched across the feasting halls.

The chariot shown on this bronze container from the fifth century B.C.E. was probably used for processions, ceremonies, and perhaps for everyday travel. Chariots of this type were the forerunners of the lightweight war chariots with which the Celts invaded much of Europe.

In 390 B.C.E. Celts and Romans met in battle at Clusium (KLOO-see-uhm), eighty miles (forty-nine kilometers) north of the city of Rome. With their tall stature, bloodcurdling war cries, swift chariots, and frenzied bravery the Celts struck terror into the well-ordered Roman legions. The Celts were victorious at Clusium and immediately headed south once more. Now they had only one goal in mind: to take Rome itself.

Eleven miles (seven kilometers) from the great city, Roman troops made a desperate attempt to stop the advancing Celts. They were horribly defeated. The citizens of Rome fled to the fortified hill of the Capitol, and the Celts marched into the wide-open city, plundering and burning it. They then besieged the Capitol for seven months. Finally the Romans paid them a tribute of one thousand pounds of gold—a tremendous sum, but it got the Celts to go back to northern Italy.

For hundreds of years afterward, the Romans vividly recalled the horror of their first meetings with the Celts. And for decades the Celts continued to live up to their terrible reputation, making repeated raids on Roman territory. These barbarians, as the Romans called them, were regarded as such a menace that in 285 B.C.E. Rome brutally exterminated an entire Celtic tribe, the Senones (seh-NOH-nays).

In 225 B.C.E. the Celts marched on Rome again. The Celtic and Roman armies met at Telamon, north of Rome. At first the Celts prevailed. But the Roman troops were far more disciplined and so were victorious in the end. It was a crushing defeat for the Celts.

At last the Romans were able to carry out their plan to rid Italy of the Celts for good. They systematically attacked and destroyed Celtic settlements, killing or driving off the inhabitants. The Celts countered with guerrilla warfare. But by 190 B.C.E. northern Italy belonged to Roman colonists, with only a few Celtic farmers remaining.

The Celts Go East

Meanwhile Greece had been having its own troubles with the Celts. By 280 B.C.E. several tribes had advanced into the Balkan region, following the Danube River eastward from the Celtic heartland. In 279 B.C.E. a force of thirty thousand warriors reached Delphi, one of the holiest places of the Greek world. There they tried to attack the temple of Apollo, the Greek sun god. But a freak blizzard, apparently followed by an earthquake, unnerved the Celts and they scattered. The Greeks took advantage of this, and the Celts suffered a grim defeat.

A Celtic warrior prepares to throw his spear (now gone). This small bronze figure, seven inches (thirteen centimeters) high, found near Rome, was made either by a Roman artist or by a Celtic artist influenced by the Romans' realistic style of sculpture.

Most of the surviving Celts escaped from Greece and settled in the Danube region. Three tribes, however, journeyed farther east. In 278 B.C.E. these groups—about twenty thousand men, women, and children in all—entered Asia Minor, where several kingdoms were vying for control of the area. The rulers of two kingdoms hired the Celts to make raids on a third kingdom. The Celts did this enthusiastically until they were defeated in 275 B.C.E. Their employers then gave them a country of their own, which became known as Galatia (from *Galatae,* a Greek name for the Celts). Celtic territory was now at its greatest extent.

The Romans Strike Back

In 125 B.C.E. a Celtic tribe attacked Massilia (present-day Marseilles, France), a wealthy Greek trading colony. A Roman army was sent to defend Massilia and soundly defeated the Celts in 124. Rome now had a foothold in the region, and by 120 B.C.E. a large area of southern Gaul (as the Romans called modern France, Belgium, and parts of Germany and Switzerland) had become a Roman province.

The next decades were extremely unsettled ones for the Celts of the European continent. They were pressured by ever more aggressive Germanic tribes in the north and by the rising Dacian culture in the east (in what is now Romania). Many tribes were on the move.

In 59 B.C.E. one tribe, the Helvetii (hel-VEH-tee-ee), left their lands in western Switzerland and headed for Gaul. To get there, however, they had to pass through Roman territory. This gave Rome a golden opportunity to send more troops against the Celts. At the head of the Roman force was the ambitious general and politician Julius Caesar. In 58 B.C.E. Caesar followed the Helvetii into Gaul, defeating them and sending most of the survivors back where they had come from.

The Romans, however, advanced into central Gaul and continued to battle the Celts. The Celtic tribes, which had a long history of fighting one another, were unable to unite against the Romans. By 56 B.C.E. Caesar had conquered all of Gaul.

In 55 and 54 B.C.E. Caesar made two brief expeditions to Britain. (These increased his heroic reputation back in Rome but seem to have made little impression on the Celts.) When he returned to Gaul, Caesar found the Celts in open rebellion. They were led by Ambiorix (am-bee-OH-rix), chief of a tribe in what is now Belgium. It took Caesar's forces a year of hard fighting to crush the uprising.

In 52 B.C.E. there was an even more serious revolt. Its leader

Caesar wrote a book describing his conquest of Gaul, but he and other Romans who described the Celts have left many questions unanswered. This scene of a man wearing a horned helmet and grasping a wheel is from the Gundestrup Cauldron, a large silver bowl that was made in the second or first century B.C.E. The Gundestrup Cauldron was found in pieces in a Danish peat bog in 1891, and scholars are still trying to solve its mysteries. It appears to illustrate several episodes from Celtic myths, but exactly what those myths were remains unknown.

was Vercingetorix (vair-kin-GEH-to-rix), whom Caesar himself described as a man of boundless energy with iron discipline. Vercingetorix almost succeeded in driving the Romans out of Gaul. But at last he, too, was defeated by Caesar. With that, the last great hope for Celtic independence in Gaul was crushed. By the time Caesar left Gaul in 50 B.C.E., he had destroyed more than eight hundred settlements and had killed or enslaved more than three million Celts.

The Last Battles

By the beginning of the Common Era, all the Celtic lands of continental Europe and Asia Minor had become part of the Roman Empire. In 43 C.E. the emperor Claudius decided to bring Britain under the empire's control as well. British resistance to the Roman invasion was fierce but disorganized—the Celts of Britain were no more united than the Celts of Gaul had been. In less than a year all of southeastern Britain fell to the Romans.

Of course, Britain was still full of tribes and leaders who hated Rome. One of these was Caratacus (ka-ruh-TAH-kus), who came from the mountainous country of western Britain and led countless raids on the Roman frontier. To put an end to this, in 47 C.E. the Roman army advanced into what is now Wales and Cornwall. They would remain there for several years, battling the Celts.

Some of the British Celts seem to have welcomed the Roman presence in their island. In 51 C.E. Cartimandua (kar-tih-MAN-doo-uh), queen of Brigantia (brih-GAN-tee-uh) in northern Britain, offered to turn her territory over to Rome. Her husband, Venutius (veh-NOO-tee-us), was defiantly anti-Roman, so Cartimandua deposed him and chose another man to rule at her side. She further proved her friendship to the Romans by luring Caratacus into a trap and then handing him over to his enemies. At this point Cartimandua's people turned against her, and she fled to Roman protection. Venutius regained his throne. The Romans would have to fight for Brigantia after all.

For the next several years the Roman army carried on campaigns in Wales. Then, around 60 C.E., the southeast arose in revolt, led by Boudicca (BOO-dih-kuh), queen of the Iceni (ee-KAY-nee).

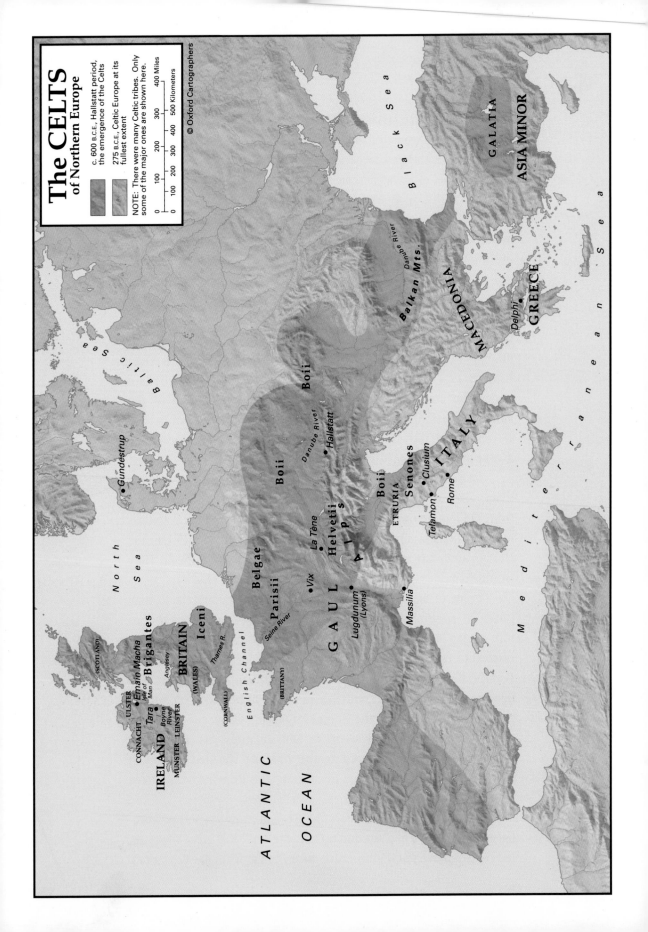

The CELTS
of Northern Europe

c. 600 B.C.E., Hallstatt period,
the emergence of the Celts

275 B.C.E. Celtic Europe at its
fullest extent

NOTE: There were many Celtic tribes. Only
some of the major ones are shown here.

0   100   200   300   400 Miles
0   100   200   300   400   500 Kilometers

© Oxford Cartographers

Baltic Sea

North Sea

Gundestrup

ATLANTIC

OCEAN

(SCOTLAND)

Emain Macha
ULSTER
Tara
CONNACHT
IRELAND
MUNSTER   LEINSTER
Boyne River
Isle of
Man

Brigantes

BRITAIN
(WALES)
Anglesey
Iceni
Thames R.

(CORNWALL)

English Channel

(BRITTANY)

Belgae

Parisii
Seine River

•Vix

G A U L
Lugdunum
(Lyons)

La Tène

Helvetii

Boii

A l p s

Massilia

Boii

Danube River
Hallstatt•

Boii

Boii

Senones
•Clusium
ETRURIA
Telamon
•Rome

ITALY

Danube River
Balkan Mts.

MACEDONIA

GREECE
Delphi•

GALATIA

ASIA MINOR

Black Sea

M e d i t e r r a n e a n   S e a

Boudicca's forces had several successes against the Romans and inflicted a huge number of casualties on them. But once again, the discipline of the Roman troops overcame the fury of the Celts. The rebellion was crushed, and Boudicca killed herself.

CELTIC QUEENS

Celtic women enjoyed an extremely high status at a very early period. This is shown by such archaeological discoveries as the grave of the "princess of Vix" in what is now eastern France. This grave contained the skeleton of a woman in her thirties who died in the late sixth century B.C.E. She was laid on a cart and surrounded by a large amount of gold and amber jewelry, along with wine vessels, bowls, and cups imported from the Mediterranean region. This kind of burial was given only to very important and powerful people.

In some situations women could rule Celtic tribes and lead warriors into battle. Even when a queen was only the wife of the tribe's ruler, she still had important rights. She was entitled to a large portion of the spoils of war and of the fines collected as penalties for crimes. The historical queens Cartimandua and Boudicca had a counterpart in the legendary Medb (mehthv) of Ireland. Though married, Medb was the undisputed ruler of the western kingdom of Connacht (KO-naht). When she decided to go to war, she herself rode in her chariot at the head of the army.

The Romans steadily continued their conquest of Britain. In 84 C.E. the island's last Celtic army was destroyed. In all of Britain, only the Highlands and Western Islands of Scotland—regarded as barren lands inhabited by wild tribes—remained free of Roman rule.

A detail from the solid gold crown that was buried with the "princess of Vix."

But across the sea to the west, there was still one independent Celtic land. Ireland preserved the ancient Celtic ways right up to the coming of Christianity in the fifth century. Even after that, many Celtic traditions persisted in Ireland for centuries more.

CHAPTER TWO

THE ART OF LIVING

This bronze plaque from northern Britain shows how Celtic artists could create a vivid image using only a few lines. The horse's faintly comical expression, as well as the clever design, would have appealed to the Celts' sense of humor.

How do we know what we know about the ancient Celts? The earliest Celts had no written language. Even when later Celts learned the Greek alphabet, they chose to use it only for such practical purposes as keeping accounts. An Irish alphabet called ogham was developed early in the Common Era, but it seems to have been used just for inscriptions on memorial stones. The Celts felt that their stories, beliefs, and history were too sacred to be written down.

Fortunately we have descriptions of the Celts from Greek and Roman writers. Indeed, much of what we know about the Celts comes from the Greeks and Romans. Their writings, however, need to be read with care. Since the Greeks and Romans regarded the Celts as their enemies, and the Celtic culture as inferior, their descriptions cannot always be believed.

Historians have learned about the Celts from other sources as well. Some of what we know comes from modern-day archaeologists, who have found and studied the numerous objects made by the Celts.

And the literature of medieval Ireland and Wales preserves many old stories and traditions. So even though the ancient Celts did not write about themselves, we still have a good picture of what they were like.

A Distinctive Appearance

The Celts were very tall and muscular, with pale skin, blond or red hair, and blue or gray eyes. Both men and women took great care with their appearance, as is shown by the fine razors, combs, and mirrors that archaeologists have found. Men in particular were

The Celts loved stories of fantastic and supernatural events, and their artwork frequently shows the same imaginative qualities. Here three heroes, accompanied by their dogs, fight three unicorns.

very careful to keep themselves slim and fit—a potbelly was a disgrace. Women used herbs to redden their cheeks and nails, and dyed their eyebrows black with berry juice.

Men and women alike took great pride in having thick, full hair, which they often curled or braided elaborately. Men sometimes used lime to bleach and stiffen their hair, which they then combed back from their foreheads. Men also generally had beards (sometimes forked or braided) and mustaches, or just mustaches, which grew freely over their mouths.

In Britain and Gaul men wore trousers and short tunics. In Ireland only servants wore trousers, while men of the upper classes wore knee-length or longer tunics, sometimes with hoods.

A reconstruction of the type of loom used by Celtic women from the eighth to the third centuries B.C.E. The warp (long) threads are held taut by polished stone weights hanging at the bottom.

Women wore tunics that reached to the ground. In all the Celtic lands, both sexes wore woolen cloaks—heavy ones in winter and light ones in summer—fastened at the neck by a brooch. These cloaks were so finely made that the Romans imported them as luxury items.

The Celts loved colorful, patterned clothing. Celtic women were expert spinners, dyers, weavers, and embroiderers. They produced beautiful linen and wool fabrics in shades of purple, blue, black, gray, green, yellow, brown, and red. Many garments were multicolored, made of striped, checked, or speckled cloth. Tunics were often fringed and elaborately decorated with embroidery. Kings, queens, and nobles sometimes had threads of gold woven into their tunics.

A bronze ornament from a wooden pitcher shows one of the hairstyles favored by Celtic men. Both the mustache and beard are curled at the ends.

Men and women alike wore a great deal of jewelry if they could afford it. Gold was the favorite material. The most distinctively Celtic piece of jewelry was the *torc,* a thick neck ring of twisted metal. Bracelets were worn on arms and wrists, and rings and anklets were common. Belts were decorated with bronze and gold ornaments.

Everyday Art

The Celts seem not to have believed much in "art for art's sake." Instead art was a regular part of their daily lives, and they lavishly decorated everything from pottery to weapons. They loved finely crafted objects that were simultaneously beautiful, useful, and frequently full of religious meaning as well. For example their jewelry was not only for adornment, but also functioned as a form of portable wealth. In addition the designs on the jewelry were often symbols to turn away evil or to bring luck and strength.

Much of Celtic art was abstract and geometrical. It could be highly stylized, eliminating most details and using only a few lines to suggest an image. Or it could be extremely complex, with elaborate decoration covering every surface of an object.

Decorated mirrors like this were especially popular in Britain in the first century B.C.E.

Popular design elements included the wheel, the spiral, and the triskele (TRY-skeel), a figure with three branches moving in the same direction around a central point. Curving, curling tendrils show that plant life was a major inspiration to Celtic artists. So were animals, which were important to the Celts for both practical and religious reasons. Sometimes artists portrayed imaginary animals, such as snakes with rams' horns and horses with wings and eagles' beaks. When the Celts

The Battersea Shield is one of the treasures of Celtic art. It is so finely decorated that it probably was not carried into battle but was saved for ceremonial occasions. Archaeologists found it in the Thames River near London.

This silver ornament from a horse's harness combines two of the most important design elements of Celtic art: the triskele and the human head.

depicted human beings, it was usually not in what we would call a realistic manner—they rarely made portraits of specific individuals. However, the human head and face were often represented, for the Celts believed that the head had great magical powers.

The Celts' greatest artistic achievements were in metalwork. While iron was used for weapons, bronze was used to make or decorate sword scabbards. Shields, of wood or leather, were often covered with beautifully worked bronze. Chariots had decorated fittings of iron, bronze, or silver. Horse harnesses had all kinds of metal ornaments. And, of course, there was the jewelry with which the Celts loved to bedeck themselves. In some of these pieces the artists worked on an incredibly small scale, making intricate designs over a surface the size of a thumbnail. Metalwork was often ornamented with enamel (usually red) and colored glass.

Sculpture in stone did not seem to have as great an importance to the Celts as metalwork did. However, many stone heads have been found throughout the Celtic lands. And as the Celts came into increasing contact with the Greeks and Romans, who had great traditions of sculpture, they were influenced to produce more artwork in stone.

Gold pinheads (the pins were probably used to fasten clothing) show the skill of Celtic metalworkers at making intricate designs even on small objects.

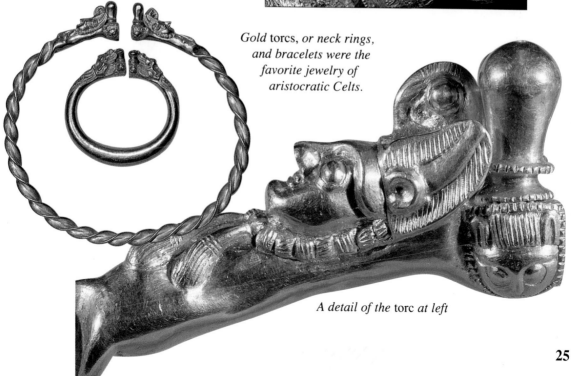

Gold torcs, *or neck rings, and bracelets were the favorite jewelry of aristocratic Celts.*

A detail of the torc *at left*

Two of the wooden statues found at the source of the Seine. They were probably offerings to Sequana, the goddess of the river.

Wood carving undoubtedly played a major role in the artistic expression of the Celts. Much of Celtic territory was heavily forested, making wood an abundant resource. The Celts also believed in the sacredness of trees, so wood was the perfect material for their religious images. In fact, archaeologists have found almost two hundred oak carvings in a single Celtic temple at the source of the Seine River, in France. Most wooden images, however, have not survived to the present.

From Forts to Feast Halls

Because warfare was such a constant condition of their lives, the Celts built a great many forts, large and small, throughout Europe. Some were simple and meant for temporary use while the population was on the move. Others were elaborate, strongly defended and intended to provide permanent shelter. Many forts were situated on top of hills or cliffs for added strength.

The Celts of continental Europe usually lived in fortified villages, called *oppida* (OH-pee-duh). In Ireland, however, and in Britain before the Romans arrived, houses were scattered over the countryside and were relatively isolated from one another. Houses in Britain, Ireland, Spain, and Portugal were round. In the rest of the Celtic lands, houses were round, oval, or rectangular.

Everywhere the houses were made of wood, sometimes also incorporating wicker, with heavy thatched or shingled roofs supported by pillars. Often these pillars were elaborately carved, as were the door lintels. Embroidered hangings sometimes decorated the walls.

In the center of the house was the hearth fire, with a smoke hole in the roof overhead. A large iron cauldron was hung over the fire, attached by a chain to one of the cross beams of the roof. Chairs seem to have been rarely used. Greek and Roman writers reported that the Celts squatted or sat cross-legged on the floor,

The Crannog Ring Fort in County Clare, Ireland, a reconstruction of ancient Celtic dwellings. A crannog was an artificial, fortified island built in a lake or marsh. Although most Celtic houses were constructed of wood, those of the Crannog Ring Fort were made of stone. The heavy thatched roofs are typical of Celtic architecture.

which was strewn with rushes or straw. Their meals were served on low wooden tables. The only other furniture may have been carved wooden chests in which valuables were stored. For beds the ancient Celts used wild-animal skins spread on the ground.

CELTIC FOOD

The Celtic lifestyle was mainly pastoral—that is, it depended on raising herds of animals. The most important animal used for food was the cow, which provided beef, milk, butter, and cheese. A person's wealth was even measured by how large his or her cattle herd was.

Meat was a major element in the diet of the Celts. They ate it fresh or preserved it with salt. It was roasted on a spit over a fire or in a cooking pit in the ground, or it was stewed in a cauldron. Beef, pork, and wild game were the favorite meats. Celts who lived near rivers or the sea also ate fish, especially salmon, which they often baked in honey. Some animals, however, were forbidden for use as food except perhaps as part of religious rituals. These animals included, in some parts of the Celtic world, hares, cranes, geese, swans, and domestic fowl.

Celtic farmers grew barley, millet, rye, oats, wheat, and beans. The grains were made into porridge or into bread that was baked in ovens or on griddles. The Celts also enjoyed fruit, such as apples and cherries.

Nobles (and some of the wealthier farmers and artisans) lived within fortified enclosures. Within the enclosure were the residence of the noble family, servants' quarters, stables, sheds, and other necessary buildings. The noble's house could be quite large, with room for many people to feast together, or there might be a separate feast hall. Inside the house, around the sides of the walls, were something like cubicles that could be screened off for privacy. In Ireland these noble houses and feast halls apparently had a second story with some sort of balcony or room that looked over the living

This reconstruction of a Celtic house's interior shows the central hearth fire and cauldron, with weapons, utensils, and farm tools arranged along the walls. On the far right is a stone hand mill, in which women (often slaves) ground grain.

space below. This was called a *grianan* (GREE-uh-nawn),* "sun-room," and seems to have been especially for women.

The Magic of Words

The Celts prized learning and intellectual accomplishments. Among the most honored members of Celtic society were the poets, called bards in Britain and Gaul and *filis* (FYIH-lyih) in Ireland.

* The Irish and Welsh languages use a number of sounds that are not used in English, so the pronunciations given in this book are often only approximate.

In this scene of a feast from the Hallstatt phase of Celtic culture, the woman on the right may be a bard reciting or a priestess performing a blessing or other ceremony.

Celtic poets had a lengthy education—the *filis,* we know, studied for seven to twelve years. The teaching was done orally, since the Celts believed that writing down their knowledge would lessen its sacredness. A master poet would sing or recite the material to be learned, and the student poets would then repeat it. In this way poets memorized vast amounts of lore, including laws, genealogies, history, stories of heroes, and myths. They were taught to play the harp or lyre, which they used to accompany their poetry, much of which was sung. They learned poetic forms and meters and various ways to use words—poets and their audiences alike delighted in detailed descriptions and subtle, elegant, clever use of language. The *filis* also learned the arts of prophecy and divination—the word *fili* meant "seer" as well as "poet."

When they "graduated," most poets became part of noble households, but they were free to travel from place to place, expecting—and usually receiving—lavish hospitality wherever they went. One of their major functions was to praise the warriors and rulers. In wartime this was an important part of the preparation for battle, building up the warriors' confidence. In peacetime the bards' praise-poetry upheld the nobles' reputations for generosity, justice, and fit behavior. But if a noble offended a bard, the bard would retaliate by composing a satirical poem about him or her, thereby ruining the noble's honorable reputation. The *filis* were believed to have such great powers that their satires could actually cause disfigurement and death. Most nobles went out of their way to treat poets well.

But the Celts did not honor poets simply out of vanity or fear. The poets were, in fact, the guardians of Celtic culture, preserving the people's traditions and passing them on from generation to generation. Performances and recitations by poets were important features of all Celtic gatherings. Stories of the births, marriages, battles, journeys, and deaths of heroes, kings, and gods were all told, probably often on corresponding occasions in the lives of ordinary Celts. Such tales, full of heroic deeds and supernatural events, provided entertainment, but also something more: They reinforced the ideals of Celtic culture and gave the Celts a strong sense of identity.

Cu Chulainn: A Hero's Tale

In Ireland at the beginning of the Common Era, some of the most popular stories were about the great hero Cu Chulainn (KOO HU-luhn). His mother was Deichtine (DYEKH-tyih-nyeh), the sister of Conchobor (KON-ho-vor), king of Ulster in northern Ireland. Deichtine became pregnant when she swallowed a small creature floating in her drink. That night the god Lugh (loo) appeared to her in a dream and told her that he was the father of the son she would bear and that she should name the child Setanta (SHAY-dan-duh).

POPULAR PASTIMES

The Celts were great lovers of competitions and games. Horse races were a major attraction at the fairs and festivals that occurred throughout the year, as were poetry and music contests.

In front of the fortresses of nobles were large fields where boys competed in team sports. The most popular of these sports was hurling, which is still played in Ireland today. It is similar to both field hockey and lacrosse. Another sport was called *baire* (BAWR-yeh), in which one team tried to get a ball into a hole in the ground while the other team defended the hole. According to Irish tales, as many as 150 boys participated in these sports at once, with the nobles as avid spectators.

The nobles themselves favored board games, especially one like chess that was called *fidchell* (FYIH-hehl) in Ireland and *gwyddbwyll* (GOO-ihth-boo-ihth) in Wales. Both words mean "wood wisdom." *Fidchell* was sometimes played just for fun, but at other times the players engaged in high-stakes gambling. Dice games were almost certainly popular as well.

Hunting, too, was a favorite pastime. Like many other activities of the Celts, it often had a religious significance. The favorite animal of the hunt was the wild boar, which was regarded as a magical beast, a gift from the deities. Several early Welsh and Irish stories tell of heroes hunting great supernatural boars.

Boar meat was a favorite food at Celtic feasts. These gatherings occurred frequently and often lasted for several days. The host of the feast generally prepared enough food so that anyone who showed up would have plenty to eat—hospitality was a sacred duty among the Celts. The host also provided a great deal of ale or Italian wine, which was drunk from a common cup passed around among the feasters as bards and jugglers provided entertainment.

When Setanta was six years old, King Conchobor asked the boy to go with him to a feast at the home of Culann (KU-lan) the blacksmith. Setanta wanted to finish the game he was playing and promised to follow after Conchobor later. Unfortunately, by the time Setanta arrived at Culann's fort, it was nearing nightfall and the blacksmith had let loose his huge, ferocious guard dog. Setanta came along, throwing his ball in front of him and catching it before it landed. The dog tore toward the boy. There was no time for anyone in the fort to rescue him. But as the hound sprang, Setanta threw his ball at its throat and killed it.

Everyone rejoiced that the boy was safe, but Culann was heartbroken by the loss of his faithful dog. Setanta then offered to act as the blacksmith's hound and guard his home and herds until one of the dead dog's puppies was full grown. A priest who was at the feast declared that from then on, Setanta would be known as Cu Chulainn, "the hound of Culann."

When Cu Chulainn grew up and it came time for him to marry, he courted a young woman named Emer (AY-ver). She first tested him by speaking to him in riddles and the secret language of the poets. Cu Chulainn easily conversed with her in this way. Emer then gave Cu Chulainn a number of feats to perform. He did them all. But Emer's father feared Cu Chulainn and, hoping that he would never come back, arranged for him to go away to study with the warrior woman Scathach (SKAW-thakh).

Scathach trained Cu Chulainn in the warrior's arts until he was skilled enough to overcome the greatest heroes in Europe. Then he returned to Ireland. Emer's father put a strong guard around her, and Cu Chulainn fought for a year to free her. At last he leaped over the triple ramparts of the fort, killed twenty-four men with three strokes of his sword, grabbed Emer, and leaped back over the ramparts with her. After that, Cu Chulainn and Emer were never parted.

CHAPTER THREE

DEITIES IN THEIR MIDST

After Rome's conquests, Celtic religion and art in Gaul and Britain came under Roman influence. This altar from Paris, sculpted in the Roman style, shows a god named Esus chopping down a tree. Although no myths about Esus survive, historians think he was probably a chieftain god—a master of warfare, building, and other useful arts.

The Celts were deeply religious. They thought of their goddesses and gods as living side by side with them in a very real way, although usually invisible to humans. Some deities were loved and admired and some were greatly feared, but all in all they were not very different from the Celts themselves. The main difference between deities and humans was that the deities simply did everything better than humans, at least partly because they had greater magical powers.

The Chieftain God and the Earth Goddess

The Celts did not have one mythology shared by all the tribes. Scholars have counted hundreds of Celtic deity names, most of which show up no more than a few times and in very limited localities. But although each tribe or region may have had its own particular names for goddesses and gods, all the Celts seem to have shared general religious ideas and to have worshiped deities of the same types.

Throughout the Celtic world, the most important deities appear to have been the chieftain god and the earth goddess. The chieftain god was often thought of as the divine ancestor, or father, of the tribe. As the tribe's special protector, he was of course a great warrior. He was also the master of all the knowledge and skills that were important to the tribe. A major chieftain god of Ireland, for example, was known as the Dagda (DAHG-thuh), the "Good God," because he was good at everything. His weapon was a club. With one end of it he could kill a person, and with the other end he

could bring the dead back to life. He owned a cauldron that was always full of the favorite food of whoever was eating from it.

The chieftain god in a sense personified, or represented in human form, the tribe that worshiped him. In the same way, the earth goddess personified the land where the tribe lived. She was identified with important natural features such as hills, springs, and rivers, all of which were sacred to the Celts. Fairs and festivals

The Celtic earth goddess had power over both birth and death, beauty and destruction. This panel from the Gundestrup Cauldron shows a goddess attended by birds and young women, with a man and a dog apparently lying dead beneath her.

35

were held in her honor. She was a mother goddess because her great concern was with fertility. Crops and herds were under her care. As protector of the land, she was also a war goddess, reigning over the battlefield and using magic to defeat her enemies.

The chieftain god had to mate with the earth goddess to ensure the prosperity of his tribe. The Dagda of Ireland mated with Boand (BOH-ahnth), "White Cow," the goddess of the Boyne River, and also with the Morrigan (MOH-ree-gahn), "Great Queen."

Often the earth goddess would seek out the mate whom she thought was most worthy. She sometimes chose kings and heroes as well as gods. She could appear to humans as young or old, beautiful or hideous. She often took on animal form.

The Goddess and the Hero

In the long tale *Tain Bo Cuailgne, The Cattle Raid of Cooley,* the Morrigan comes to the hero Cu Chulainn as a beautiful maiden dressed in multicolored clothes. She offers him her treasure, her cattle, and her love. Cu Chulainn, however, is defending Ulster single-handed and tells the Morrigan that he has no time for a woman right now. The goddess then offers him her help, but when he rejects her again, she vows to hinder him instead.

Later, when the hero is fighting a heated single combat in the middle of a river, the Morrigan takes the form of an eel and coils around his feet. He loses his balance and falls, and his enemy is able to wound him several times. Cu Chulainn manages to get up again, smashes the eel's ribs, and the battle resumes. Next the Morrigan becomes a wolf and attacks Cu Chulainn. He drives her off by slinging a stone at her and blinding her in one eye. Finally the goddess appears as a red cow and stampedes a herd of cattle through the river where the hero is fighting. He slings another stone and breaks her legs.

Cu Chulainn at last kills his enemy, but he is at the end of his strength. He sees an old woman milking a cow and asks her for a drink of milk. She gives it to him and he blesses her. He asks for a second and a third drink, and each time the woman grants his request, he blesses her again. Then the woman reveals that she is the Morrigan and that Cu Chulainn's three blessings have healed her of the three injuries he gave her.

Like many Celtic goddesses, the Morrigan often appeared as a trinity, or group of three. She was frequently accompanied by the battle goddesses Nemain (NEH-vuhn), "Panic," and Badb (bahthv), "Crow." The number three was sacred to the Celts. Anything multiplied by three was especially powerful. There are

A Romano-British sculpture of the Mothers—Celtic goddesses of fruitfulness and plenty.

THE FOUR FESTIVALS

The Irish Celts had four great holy days. Some of these, at least, were also celebrated in Britain and Gaul, and perhaps elsewhere in the Celtic world.

The first and most important festival, Samhain (SAH-wuhn), was celebrated from sundown October 31 to sundown November 1. The holiday marked the beginning of both winter and the new year. In Irish tales it was at Samhain that kings and heroes underwent supernatural tests or met their fated deaths. During Samhain there was closer contact between the otherworld and the human world than at any other time of the year. Our modern holidays of Halloween and All Saints' Day had their beginnings in the Celtic festival of Samhain.

Imbolc (IM-bohlg), January 31 to February 1, was the beginning of spring. Ewes were now milked for the first time, and preparations for planting probably started. The goddess Brigit was particularly connected with this festival.

Summer began with Beltine (BYEHL-tyih-nyeh), celebrated April 30 to May 1. On this day cattle were driven between two bonfires to bless them before they went out to their summer pastures.

The last holiday of the year was Lughnasadh (LOO-nah-sah), the festival of the god Lugh. Celebrated July 31 to August 1, this was the beginning of autumn and harvesttime.

For all these festivals, except perhaps Imbolc, the Irish Celts gathered in large numbers at ceremonial centers throughout the island. These special holy places were named after earth goddesses, who were usually said to have died or been buried there. In Ulster, for example, Lughnasadh was celebrated at Emain Macha (EH-vuhn MAH-huh), where the goddess Macha gave birth to twins and died after beating the king's horses in a race. Women's footraces were a special feature of this particular Lughnasadh celebration.

The holiday gatherings were both sacred and festive. There were religious rites, marketplaces, games and contests, and performances of music and poetry. But perhaps the most special thing about these days for the Celts was that no one was permitted to behave violently in any way.

many stone carvings from Britain and Gaul showing triple goddesses, especially those called the Mothers, who are shown with children, fruit, or loaves of bread. One of the most important Irish deities was Brigit (BRIH-ghyihd), who was sometimes thought of as being three sisters of the same name. One sister was specially concerned with poetry and prophecy, one with healing, and the third with smithcraft and metalwork.

Masters of the Arts

The earth goddess and the chieftain god were sometimes related to other deities. Brigit, the Morrigan, and the Dagda all belonged to a family of deities descended from the goddess Danu (DA-noo). The group was called the Tuatha De Danann (TOO-ah-thuh dyay DAH-nuhn), "Tribes of the Goddess Danu." In Wales there was a similar family of deities whose mother was called Don. Both names may be related to the Danube River, a major pathway of Celtic migration.

Many of the children of Danu and Don were goddesses and gods that had particular specialties or occupations. They were probably regarded as "patron saints" of people who worked at those occupations. There was a divine blacksmith, called Goibniu (GOV-nyoo) in Ireland and Govannon (go-VAH-nuhn) in Wales. The Irish Credne (CRAYTH-nyeh) was a metalworker, and Luchta (LUKH-duh) was a carpenter. Dian Cecht (DYEE-uhn KYAYKHT), his two sons, and his daughter were doctors. The Welsh Amaethon (uh-MY-thuhn) was a patron of farmers, and his brother Gwydion (goo-ih-DEE-ohn) was a master wizard. The Tuatha De Danann also had wizards, as well as poets, historians, cupbearers, doorkeepers, harp players, and, of course, warriors.

One day when the Tuatha De Danann were at the fort of Tara feasting with their king, Nuada (NOO-ah-thuh), a handsome

Caesar wrote that one of the major Celtic deities was one who resembled Minerva, the Roman goddess of war and of arts and crafts. The goddess portrayed in this bronze head from Gaul wears a helmet inspired by the type of helmet worn by Minerva, but the goose crest is purely Celtic. This goddess was probably related to the Irish Brigit.

39

stranger arrived at the gate. The doorkeeper asked who he was and what art he practiced, "for no one without an art enters Tara." The stranger, Lugh, said that he was a builder, but the doorkeeper replied that they did not need a builder since they had one of their own. Lugh then said that he was a blacksmith, but, of course, there was a smith at Tara, too. Lugh named all of his arts, but every one of them was already practiced by some member of the Tuatha De Danann. At last Lugh said, "Ask the king whether he has one man who possesses all these arts."

When Nuada heard about the stranger at the gate, he exclaimed, "A man like that has never before come into this fortress." Lugh was admitted to Tara, where the feasters demanded that he play the harp for them. He played sleep music so that everyone there slept for the next twenty-four hours. After that he played sorrowful music until everyone was weeping and lamenting. He finished by playing joyful music, and everyone laughed and rejoiced. Because of his many powers, Lugh was not only welcomed among the Tuatha De Danann but became one of their leaders.

The many-talented Lugh, who embodied all the traits most admired by the Celts, was one of the best-loved Celtic deities. In

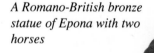

A Romano-British bronze statue of Epona with two horses

Wales he was known as Lleu (TLEH-ee) and in continental Europe as Lugos (LOO-gohs). Many European cities were originally named after him, including Carlisle, England; Legnica, Poland; and Lyons, France.

The Horse Goddess and the Horned God

Only a few deities besides Lugh were worshiped over more than a small portion of the Celtic world. One was the goddess of horses, who seems to have been honored by nearly all the Celts. In Gaul she was known as Epona, meaning "mare." She became the favorite deity of the Roman cavalry, which spread her worship throughout the Roman Empire.

The most popular Celtic god of all seems to have been the horned god, usually referred to as Cernunnos (ker-NU-nohs). Numerous images of the horned god have been found throughout the Celtic world, and there were a

Crowned with antlers and surrounded by animals and foliage, the horned god holds a torc *and a ram-headed snake in this scene from the Gundestrup Cauldron.*

variety of names for him. He is generally depicted with deer antlers on his head, symbolizing virility and strength. Often he holds a bag with coins pouring out of it. Animals frequently accompany him, including ram-headed snakes. These images show that the horned god was a deity of hunting, fertility, and wealth. It may be that the horned god, clearly a provider of the necessities of life, was

SACRED ANIMALS

One of the ways in which the deities of the Celts were believed to mingle with humans was in animal form. For this reason animals were regarded with great reverence. Many animals were sacred in their own right as well.

The animals with the greatest religious significance were the boar, stag, bull, horse, and dog. The boar was the supreme Celtic animal, believed to embody all the virtues of the warrior. Boar meat was also considered to be the food of the gods, and so it was the favorite food at Celtic feasts. Like the boar, the stag was an important animal for hunting. In myths, magical stags frequently lured humans into the divine realms. Bulls represented strength and fertility, as well as the central role of cattle in the Celtic economy. Horses—both mares and stallions—were connected with many deities and symbolized, among other things, the sun, fertility, the earth, and war. Dogs had connections with healing, hunting, and the duty of the hero to guard the tribal lands and herds.

Birds played a major role in Celtic belief, from the tiny wren to the majestic eagle. Birds were messengers of the gods and were closely observed. Their behavior, calls, and flight patterns were interpreted to predict the future. The Welsh goddess Rhiannon (rhee-AH-nuhn) had three magical birds whose wondrous singing could lull the living to sleep and bring the dead back to life. The birds considered most sacred by the Celts were the swan and the raven. The swan was regarded as a bird of love, beauty, purity, and magical music. The raven was a bird of wisdom and prophecy as well as of death and destruction. Because ravens fed on the corpses on battlefields, they were especially associated with war goddesses.

Even some fish, particularly the salmon, were sacred to the Celts. In early Irish tales salmon are among the oldest animals in the world and have witnessed all the ages of humanity. Irish tradition also told of the salmon of knowledge, who swam in a clear pool and ate magical hazelnuts that fell into the water. Anyone who caught and ate one of these salmon would be filled with wisdom and be able to foresee all future events.

The White Horse of Uffington is a monument to the ancient Celts' devotion to the horse. It was carved into this hillside in southern England probably between the first century B.C.E. and the first century C.E., its makers cutting through the turf to reveal the chalk beneath. The White Horse measures 365 feet (110 meters) from nose to tail.

another form of the chieftain god. Unfortunately, as with so many other Celtic deities, no clear myths about him have survived to the present.

The Otherworld

To the ancient Celts, the realm of the deities was a completely real place. It existed side by side with the human world. Communication between the divine and human worlds was common and could occur without warning. For example, in the Welsh tale of Pwyll (POO-ihth), the hero goes out hunting and suddenly finds himself in a part of the forest he's never seen before, where he meets Arawn (AH-rown), a king of the otherworld. Later in the story Pwyll is sitting on top of a mound when out of nowhere appears the goddess Rhiannon riding a white horse that no other horse can catch up with.

Sometimes the otherworld was thought of as being underground, entered through caves or burial mounds, or underwater. It was probably for this reason that the ancient Celts threw thousands of precious objects—such as jewelry, swords, shields, coins, and cauldrons—into lakes, ponds, rivers, and wells. Sometimes they buried large amounts of treasure in deep shafts in the ground.

The otherworld was also thought of as an island or group of islands reached by sailing west over the sea. The Irish had many names for such islands: the Land of Promise, the Plain of Honey, the Land of the Young, the Island of Women, the Island of Joy, the Many-Colored Land.

The otherworld was a beautiful, joyful place where there was always wonderful music and never illness, death, sorrow, or treachery.

We do not know for certain if the Celts believed that they would join the deities in the otherworld after death, although this seems likely. Celtic nobles were buried with many of their precious possessions and objects they used in their daily lives—everything from weapons and jewelry to cauldrons and chariots. This indicates that the Celts did believe in a real, physical afterlife. Feasting was definitely a part of this afterlife, too, for joints of pork were often buried with the dead.

Perhaps the otherworld feast was just one of many stops on the soul's journey after death. According to Caesar, the Celts believed that the souls of the dead were reborn into new bodies. Some early Welsh and Irish literature does seem to bear out such a belief in reincarnation. For example stories of the great Welsh bard Taliesin (tal-ee-EH-sin) described how he had had many existences throughout the ages: "I have been dead, I have been alive, I am Taliesin."

The ancient Celts admired the strength and ferocity of the wild boar and preferred its meat for their feasts. It was the most challenging and dangerous animal to hunt, and according to surviving myths, it might lead the hunter into the otherworld.

CHAPTER FOUR

THE CELTIC IDEAL IN PRACTICE

The deities of the Celts possessed all of the qualities that the people as a whole admired and desired. They were the divine reflection of Celtic society both as it was and as it aspired to be. Halfway between gods and humans were semidivine heroes such as Cu Chulainn. They represented the ideals of individual bravery, physical strength, intellectual ability, and spiritual energy. In the human world the Celtic people did their best to live by these values, led and inspired by their priests and rulers.

This ax, decorated with a horse and rider, was found at Hallstatt. It was probably used in religious ceremonies.

Druids

The Celtic priests of Ireland, Britain, and Gaul, who often held their rituals in groves of sacred oak trees, were called druids, which means something like "wise men of the oak." They had many functions in Celtic society, all of which, in one way or another, helped to keep the people in the proper relationship with the divine. Along with conducting religious ceremonies, the druids were teachers, healers, prophets, judges, lawyers, royal advisers, and astronomers. It took up to twenty years of study to become a druid.

The druids were highly respected and had many privileges. In assemblies, no one—not even the king—could speak before the druids spoke. They did not have to pay taxes and were exempt from military training and service.

Druids were so powerful that they could stop a battle between two tribes simply by standing between the opposing armies. If an individual or even a whole tribe disobeyed the druids' rulings, they banned the offender from attending religious ceremonies. A person placed under the druids' ban was completely shut out of the life of the community.

From inside the Gundestrup Cauldron comes this mysterious image. Some scholars interpret it as a scene of human sacrifice, while others say that it shows a god allowing a mortal man to drink from a divine cauldron. A third possibility is that the image depicts a ritual somewhat like baptism.

One function of the druids was to oversee rituals of sacrifice. As in most of the ancient world, animal sacrifice was frequently performed. On some occasions the Celts also practiced human sacrifice. Caesar wrote that when a Celtic tribe was in especially great danger, a gigantic human image would be woven of wicker, and criminals would be burned to death in it.

Archaeologists found proof of Celtic human sacrifice when they discovered the well-preserved body of "Lindow Man" in a peat bog in England. Lindow Man was clearly a noble—perhaps even a druid—and he had been stabbed and strangled, and had had his throat cut, before being thrown into the bog. This kind of "triple death," archaeologists believe, is evidence of a ritual sacrifice.

Archaeologists have also found many human skeletons, bones, and skulls buried under or near Celtic dwellings. The purpose of these bones seems to have been to give spiritual strength and protection to the places where they were buried. But it is not certain that all of these people were ritually killed. Some of them may have died of natural causes but have been so beloved or revered that they were buried in this special way.

Roman writers described the Celts' practice of human sacrifice with great horror. In fact human sacrifice had been illegal in Rome for only a hundred years or so—and a favorite form of Roman entertainment was to go to the arena and watch people being killed in various ways. But Roman generals were able to use human sacrifice as a reason to destroy the powerful druidic priesthood. And they did so ruthlessly, even burning down the holy oak groves. In 61 C.E., for example, Roman troops massacred a large number of British druids at their sacred center on the island of Anglesey, off the coast of Wales. The real reason for Roman opposition to the druids was probably that the priesthood was the one force capable of uniting the Celtic tribes to resist the invaders.

Kings

To the Celts, their kings were sacred and nearly divine. They were chosen with elaborate ritual. In Ireland, for example, when a king was to be chosen, a bull was sacrificed and cooked. One man—probably a druid, but perhaps a *fili*—ate and drank his fill of the beef and broth. He then lay down to sleep on the bull's skin, and other druids or *filis* chanted an "incantation of truth" over him so that his dreams would reveal who the new king should be. If he lied about what he dreamed, he would die.

A Celtic king took office with great ceremony, during which he was symbolically married to the earth goddess. It was believed that the king had a crucial relationship to the land—if he was weak, infertile, unjust, or ruled unwisely, the crops would fail and the cows would stop giving milk. Every aspect of the tribe's well-being depended on the fitness of the king.

The king was not all-powerful, and he could be removed from office. This could be done if he fathered no children, if he was maimed, if he lost a war, or for other reasons. He was expected to abide by the wishes of his people, even in his personal life. When he grew old and his health began to fail, he may have been ritually killed so that his loss of strength would not affect the strength of the tribe and the fertility of the land.

Nobles and Commoners

By the time of Caesar's conquest in 58 B.C.E., many of the Celtic tribes of Gaul no longer had kings. Instead they had officials who were elected at annual assemblies. These officials ruled along with the nobles. Throughout its history Celtic society remained highly aristocratic.

Nobles were wealthy property owners who had large numbers of clients. A client was a freeman who promised certain services to a more influential freeman. Clients provided food, manual labor, hospitality, and military service in return for protection and other kinds of assistance. Clients took loans from their lords and paid them back with interest. So the more clients a noble had, the richer and more powerful he became. An ordinary freeman also could improve his status by taking on clients. If his family maintained its wealth and clients, his grandson could then become a noble. It is not certain whether women participated in this system of clientship.

The ties among nobles were strengthened by the practice of fosterage. Lesser nobles sent their children to be raised and educated by more powerful nobles. Children and foster parents formed very close relationships, and the bond between foster brothers was regarded as nearly sacred.

Because of their religious role and their great learning, druids and poets were part of the noble class whether they were born into it or not (although they usually were). Ancient Celtic society—at least in Ireland—also allowed individuals to move from a lower class to a higher one if they were particularly talented in some art or craft.

Beneath the nobles were the free farmers and artisans. Craftspeople were greatly honored and respected by the Celts. The

A cow and her calf form the handle of this bronze ladle discovered at Hallstatt. Celtic artisans, who were highly respected, made even the most ordinary items works of art.

blacksmith's rank seems to have been especially high, partly because of the importance of weapons in this warlike culture. But more than that, the craft of forging iron was seen to have a magical, supernatural character, and so the blacksmith was someone with a special relationship to the divine.

The majority of the people in the Celtic world were little better than slaves. They probably did most of the agricultural work on the lands of the upper classes, but they possessed no land of their own. They had no voice in the tribal assemblies, and they were not allowed to bear arms. Actual slavery also existed among the Celts. Female slaves seem to have performed most of the heavy domestic chores in the households of the upper classes.

Warriors

With the exception of the druids, every Celtic freeman was a warrior in addition to any other occupation he might follow. Among the Celts, a state of war was considered normal and was even desirable. It seems that just about the only time the Celts would avoid a fight was when the druids had declared that the month or day was unlucky for conflict.

Celtic warfare took many forms, from raids by relatively small war bands to great battles in which entire tribes were involved. In Ireland, according to stories, raids were particularly carried out by special war bands called *fiana* (FYEE-uh-nuh). A warrior who wanted to join a *fian* had to undergo extremely difficult physical tests and also had to be well educated in poetry. Once accepted into a *fian,* the warrior broke all ties with his (or occasionally her) family and tribe. But although the *fiana* were outside of tribal life, they had a recognized role in Irish society. They spent the summer living mainly outdoors, hunting and plundering, and in the winter, it seems, they received the hospitality of nobles and commoners alike.

This horned helmet was discovered in the Thames River in England. It may have been made specifically as an offering, thrown into the river, either to ask the gods for success in battle or to thank them for a victory.

The Celts were especially fearsome in battle. The highest-ranking warriors fought in chariots or, in Gaul by the time of Caesar's conquest, on horseback. Before the battle began, they would ride wildly back and forth in front of the enemy, boasting of their own strength and heroism and hurling insults at their foes. There were probably druids—and many individual warriors—loudly praying to the deities for success and glory. Added to all this shouting was the braying of great animal-headed war trumpets

called *carnyxes*. This incredible noise was designed to confuse and panic the enemy, and it frequently succeeded in doing so.

Perhaps it was because Celtic warriors were so sure that life continued after death that they fought without regard to their personal safety. Some even went into battle naked. Others wore iron breastplates of chain mail, and many had bronze helmets with

horns or animal figures projecting from them. They whipped themselves up into such a frenzy that their physical appearance was often distorted. In Britain warriors made themselves look still more inhuman and terrifying by painting their faces blue with dye from the woad plant.

Celtic warriors especially enjoyed engaging in single combat.

Accompanied by three carnyx *players, foot soldiers march toward the mysterious figure with the cauldron. Warriors on horseback, led by a ram-headed snake, ride away.*

This was the type of fighting in which a hero won the greatest glory. When two Celtic tribes fought each other, each side would put forward champions to offer single combat to the warriors of the other side. The strong Celtic code of honor required that a warrior who offered single combat should be fought only by a single opponent.

These fights usually took place at the ford of a river or stream. The two champions faced each other from opposite sides of the water and began by showing off their feats of arms. They bragged about themselves and insulted and threatened each other. Once their battle fury was stirred up, they met in the ford, fighting with swords or with thrusting-spears. Their charioteers and other warriors stood behind them, urging them on. The winner of the single combat usually beheaded his dead opponent and attached the head to his chariot or saddle as a sign of his victory.

The Celts also engaged in single combat at their feasts. Often

THE SACRED HEAD

To the Celts the head was the most important part of the human body. The head was the seat of the eternal soul and so was symbolic of life after death. It had divine powers. When Celtic warriors took the heads of their enemies, they were doing more than showing off their skill in battle. The warrior who acquired the head of his enemy acquired his enemy's strength. The severed head also had great powers of protection, and it would be impaled on a stake in front of the house or fortress of the victorious warrior. In southern France, archaeologists have found the remains of Celtic temples with niches in the walls to hold human heads—there were some skulls still in place. Even a representation of the human head had the ability to summon divine power and turn away evil. Images of human heads therefore decorated everything from weapons to jewelry.

The early Welsh tale of Bran (brahn) son of Llyr (tleer) gives a good picture of Celtic beliefs about the sacred head. When Bran was seriously wounded in battle in Ireland, he asked his men to behead him. After his head was struck off, it still had the power of speech. Following Bran's instructions, the men returned to Wales. There they feasted for eighty-seven years, during which they never grew any older. Bran's head remained undecayed and was as pleasant company as Bran had been in life, and the men never had a more joyous time. When the feasting came to an end, the men took Bran's head to the White Mount in London and buried it there to protect the island of Britain from invasion.

A reconstruction of the entrance to a Celtic temple in southern France. When archaeologists found these ruins, the skulls were still in place in their niches.

these combats started out as mock battles or drills. But a great deal of wine and ale was drunk at feasts, and the warriors might easily lose control and begin to fight in earnest. Sometimes death or serious injury resulted if no one stepped in to stop the combat. Another potential cause of violence was the Celts' custom of awarding the best piece of meat, the "hero's portion," to the greatest warrior at a feast. Quarrels over who deserved the hero's portion were quite likely to end up in fights to the death. In this case the warrior's honor and reputation were at stake, and there was little the Celts valued more than these two things.

Women

With its strong emphasis on warfare, one might expect that Celtic society would not give a very important place to women. In fact it seems that Celtic women enjoyed many rights and a wide range of roles. One important sign of the high status of women among the Celts was that the last names of gods and heroes often included their mothers' names.

The laws of early medieval Ireland may reflect ancient Celtic customs. According to these laws, a woman had the right to choose her husband and could not be married without her consent. When she married, she did not become part of her husband's family and she continued to own her own property, which could include anything from clothes and jewelry to cattle herds. If she and her husband were equal in rank and wealth, she could enter into contracts without her husband's permission and could even cancel her husband's contracts if they were unwise. If her fortune was greater than her husband's, she was the undisputed head of the family. If her husband took a second wife or a concubine (a legally recognized mistress), the first wife was automatically entitled to financial compensation or a divorce. Divorce was easily obtained for a number of reasons, and a woman took with her all of the personal property she brought into the marriage and anything she acquired during it. She could remarry as many times as she liked.

Celtic women could be craftspeople, healers, and poets. This was reflected in the myths and legends of the Celts. Among the Tuatha De Danann, the goddess Cron (krone) worked with the

IF YOU LIVED IN CELTIC EUROPE

If you had been born into an ancient Celtic family, your way of life would have been determined by the facts of your birth—whether you were a girl or a boy, slave or free, wealthy or poor. With this chart you can trace the course your life might have taken as a member of the Celtic aristocracy.

You were born into the Celtic nobility. . . .

As a Boy . . .

As a Girl . . .

At a young age you go to live with a higher-ranking noble family. Your foster parents care for you deeply, and you are very close to your foster siblings.

During fosterage you are taught to swim, ride horses, play games of strategy, and fight with various weapons. You play team sports with other boys. You learn tribal lore and poetry from druids and *filis*. You may begin training to become a poet or a druid.

When you are 17 you return to your parents. You are ready to be given weapons of your own; this probably occurs in a special ritual. You are now officially a warrior, and you can get married. You may also have one or more concubines, but only with your wife's approval.

As an adult you make yourself a client of a higher-ranking noble, and you take on clients of your own. You spend a great deal of time practicing your feats of arms. You go to war frequently and sometimes take part in raids on neighboring tribes. You attend rituals and tribal gatherings. You host and attend feasts. You enjoy playing board games and hunting. You foster your clients' sons and train them to become warriors.

During fosterage you are taught to weave, sew, and embroider. You are probably also taught to swim and ride, and you learn some fighting skills. You learn tribal lore and poetry from druids and *filis*. You may begin training to become a poet or priestess.

When you are 14 you return to your parents. You can now be married if you choose to. If you do, you remain financially and legally independent. You can divorce your husband for good reason and can remarry as many times as you like.

As an adult much of your time is spent producing cloth and clothing. You are assisted by female slaves and, if you are married, by any concubines your husband has. You may own a herd of cattle and have other business interests. When your tribe is at war, you are ready to defend your home and may actually go into battle. You attend rituals, feasts, and tribal gatherings. You care for and help to educate your foster children.

In old age, you are a respected elder of the tribe. When you die, your passing is lamented with wailing and keening. Your body may be cremated, exposed to the elements, or buried, often with food and drink and many precious possessions.

smith god Goibniu, sharpening the weapons he forged. The goddess Airmed (AR-myehth) was a highly skilled physician. The triple goddess Brigit was a smith, a physician, and, above all, a poet.

This evidently powerful goddess (portrayed on the Gundestrup Cauldron) is a reminder of the esteem with which women were regarded in Celtic culture.

Women poets were often also prophets, and Celtic women may have taken other religious roles as well. Greek and Roman writers described groups of priestesses who lived on islands and were healers and prophets. When the Romans attacked the druid shrine at Anglesey, there were wild-haired women with flaming torches running among the druids and warriors, screaming curses at the invaders. It is not known for certain if the women in these examples were part of the druid order. The women of Anglesey may have been the wives and daughters of the druids there. The island priestesses could have been women druids, or members of a religious order that was for women only—or the Greek and Roman authors could have misunderstood a myth about the otherworld Island of Women. Still, it seems likely that the Celts had priestesses of some kind.

There is no doubt that Celtic women often took an active part in warfare. When the whole tribe went to war, women protected the baggage carts, livestock, and most especially the children. Some women fought in the forefront of battle. In Ireland, a woman who had received cattle or land from the king was obligated to provide military service in return. Women could join the *fiana*.

The wives of Celtic warriors seem to have always been ready to fight side by side with their husbands, as one Roman writer described: "A whole band of foreigners will be unable to cope with one Celt in a fight if he calls in his wife, stronger than he by far and with flashing eyes; least of all when she swells her neck and gnashes her teeth, and poising her huge white arms, begins to rain blows mingled with kicks like shots discharged by the twisted cords of a catapult."

CHAPTER FIVE

A LIVING CULTURE

B y the end of the first century C.E., the Celts of Britain and the European continent had lived for several generations under Roman rule and were becoming romanized. By the third century they were being Christianized as well. Traditional Celtic culture, however, still managed to hang on to a fair extent in remote areas of Britain, away from the Roman cities and villas. The Celts of Ireland, meanwhile, were untouched by Rome and continued to live according to their age-old beliefs and customs well into the fifth century. Then Christianity arrived in Ireland, and there, too,

In medieval Ireland, Christian monasteries like this one preserved much of the artistic and literary heritage of the ancient Celts.

the ancient ways began to alter. But whatever changes came, the Celtic people and their culture were destined, in one form or another, to survive.

The Last Celtic Strongholds

In 410 C.E. the Roman Empire pulled out of Britain, and the British Celts found themselves independent once more. These were troubled times, however. For many years Irish raiders had been attacking western Britain. Some of them had settled there, especially in southwest Wales. The romanized British were even more threatened by the Picts (a Celtic people about whom little is known), who were relentlessly pushing southward from what is now Scotland.

To the ancient Celts, springs, wells, and the sources of rivers were especially holy places. In the Celtic countries today, holy wells, such as this one in County Donegal, Ireland, continue to be special places at which to pray. The wells are usually dedicated to the Virgin Mary or to Saint Brigit, who closely resembles the ancient goddess Brigit. Worshipers leave flowers, small gifts, and rags tied to nearby bushes to give thanks for the saints' help.

British leaders turned to the Saxons of Germany for help. The Saxons were given land in Britain in exchange for fighting off the Picts. But the Saxons soon turned against the British, attacking and burning farms and settlements all across the southern portion of the island. They received boatload after boatload of reinforcements, including groups of Angles, also from Germany. Within a hundred years, the Saxons and Angles—known together as the Anglo-Saxons—were in complete control of a large part of Britain. They called their territory Angle Land—England. In this region Anglo-Saxon culture wiped out virtually all of Celtic culture that had survived the Romans.

The British Celts were pushed back into the westernmost portions of the island, Wales and Cornwall. But here they were

THE IRISH CHURCH

The Irish were converted to Christianity relatively quickly and easily, perhaps because their ancient religion was open to so many different ideas about the divine. Irish Christians were also very flexible. They adapted some elements of their native culture to Christianity and some elements of Christianity to their native culture. Monasticism—groups of religious men or women living in communities—was central to Irish Christianity. Early Irish monasteries were probably modeled on the schools where the druids taught.

The monasteries produced works of art that continued and developed the traditional Celtic style. Monks spent many hours every day producing and copying books by hand. They decorated these manuscripts with wonderful illuminations, or illustrations, using complicated interlacing designs and depicting all kinds of fantastic animals. Elaborately carved stone crosses were erected on the grounds of the monasteries. Frequently these were adorned with the same sort of patterns seen in ancient Celtic metalwork.

Irish monks were enthusiastic missionaries. They traveled throughout Europe, establishing monasteries in many places besides their homeland. Wherever they were located, Irish monasteries were places of tremendous intellectual activity. Indeed, during the early Middle Ages, when much of Europe was in complete chaos, Irish monks were responsible for preserving a great deal of the learning of the ancient world.

met by Irish invaders. In the fifth and sixth centuries, many British Celts left Wales and Cornwall and settled in northwestern Gaul. Like Britain, much of Gaul was overrun by Germanic tribes. But the British were able to maintain their foothold, and their new territory became known as Brittany.

During the same period, Irish power continued to expand. Irish settlers from Ulster founded the kingdom of Dalriada (dawl-REE-ah-thuh) in northwestern Britain. This was the beginning of the nation of Scotland, which took its name from the Irish colonists, who were called Scotti. There was also a strong Irish presence in the Isle of Man (named after the sea god Manannan), located in the Irish Sea between Ireland and northern England.

Wales, Cornwall, Brittany, Ireland, Scotland, and the Isle of Man were the last strongholds of Celtic culture. They were good strongholds too, standing up through centuries more of foreign conquests, attacks, and influences. In some of these areas ancient Celtic institutions lasted almost unchanged until fairly recent times. Ireland had *filis* and bards throughout the Middle Ages. Until the eighteenth century, Scottish society was organized in clans that functioned and behaved just like the Celtic tribes of long ago. Modern Scots are still proud of their clan membership.

This early medieval Irish stone cross is carved with scenes from the Bible and the lives of saints but still retains connections with the pre-Christian past: The ring uses the same kind of designs found in ancient Celtic metalwork, and at the base of the cross are two chariots.

From Oral Tradition to World Literature

"It is said of the hero Fionn MacCumhaill [FYUN mac-KOO-wuhl] that if a day goes by without his name being mentioned the world will come to an end." Fionn was the legendary leader of the most renowned *fian* in Ireland. He was said to have died around 250 C.E. But the quoted sentence is not from some ancient manuscript. It is from the beginning of a story told by twentieth-century Scottish musician and storyteller Robin Williamson. Like the Celtic bards of long ago, Williamson recites the old poems and tales to the accompaniment of his harp. Unlike them, he does so not only in live performances but also on compact disk and videotape.

Celtic stories from nearly two thousand years ago have survived to the present largely because of the thoroughly trained memories of the ancient bards and *filis*. These people were living libraries, entrusted to guard and preserve the lore and learning of their culture. Then Roman conquest and Christianity brought a change in intellectual attitudes: Gradually knowledge became something to be written down in books rather than passed on orally from generation to generation. Fortunately the poets of Wales and especially of Ireland kept their oral literature alive long enough for much of it to be turned into written literature.

The people who wrote down the old stories were not bards or *filis* themselves. They were mostly Christian monks, and there were large portions of the ancient material that they did not understand, approve of, or perhaps remember correctly. Often they added elements of Christianity or foreign ideas to the tales they recorded. Still, we are very lucky that they realized the ancient literature was worth preserving and that they made their best effort to do so.

One other force was responsible for keeping alive stories of the great Celtic heroes, and that was the ordinary people of the countryside. The lifestyle of these peasants changed very little from

Scottish musician and storyteller Robin Williamson brings the wit and beauty of Celtic myths and folktales to enthusiastic audiences across the United States, Canada, and Europe.

The Celtic art style continued to develop in the monasteries of early medieval Britain and Ireland, where monks produced elaborately decorated books of the Gospels and other Christian scriptures. This illumination from the ninth century Book of Kells combines complex interlacing with such ancient Celtic designs as spirals, triskeles, and even human heads.

the first centuries of the Common Era to the early twentieth century. Even when there were no more poets singing the ancient lore in
the halls of the nobles, storytellers at cottage firesides upheld the
tradition of oral literature. Alongside newer tales, some ultimately
from foreign sources, the deeds of Fionn MacCumhaill and his
fiana continued to be celebrated. The old deities were remembered,
too, although now they had become saints, demons, witches and
wizards, kings and queens, or fairies.

In the twelfth century, ancient Celtic deities and heroes, often
with new names, entered upper-class European literature in the stories of King Arthur. Historians believe that Arthur was originally a
British war leader who fought the invading Saxons in the fifth or
sixth century. He became a great hero in north Britain, Wales, and
Cornwall. His legend grew steadily, bringing in a wide range of
mythological elements. For example many of the deeds of Celtic

THE LORE OF THE FAIRIES

The Celtic people did not immediately and completely give up their ancient beliefs
when they accepted Christianity. Many beliefs gradually changed into forms that
were able to coexist with the new religion. And so a number of the old deities came to
be thought of as fairies.

A Welsh name for the fairies, *y mamau* (uh MA-my), means "the mothers," a
reminder of the earth goddess of the Celts. In Irish the fairies were usually called the
sidh (shee), "the people of the mounds," because they were believed to live in ancient
burial mounds.

Like the deities of the Celts, the fairies moved among humans both invisibly and vis-
ibly, often taking animal form. They could change size but usually appeared human-sized.
(The idea of fairies as tiny, delicate beings seems to have come from William
Shakespeare's sixteenth-century play *A Midsummer Night's Dream*.) These fairies were
aristocratic: They lived like Celtic nobles, enjoying music, feasting, hunting, fighting, and
splendid processions. Other types of fairy folk—such as leprechauns, brownies, pixies,
and bogles—seem to be descended from nature spirits that were worshiped by the
peasants, perhaps as far back as pre-Celtic times. Some of these spirits were quite dangerous to humans. But many types of fairies often helped deserving individuals.

Belief in the fairies, especially in rural Ireland, remained strong until well into the
twentieth century. And although there may be few believers left today, the fairy lore of
the Celtic lands continues to inspire the imaginations of children and adults alike.

A vision of the Holy Grail appears to King Arthur and his knights in this illumination from a fifteenth-century French manuscript.

gods were now said to have been performed by Arthur. Gods and heroes from both Britain and Ireland were named among his knights, including Lugh. Arthur received a magical sword from a fairy called the Lady of the Lake, who was very much like the ancient earth goddess. The Holy Grail that Arthur's knights quested after was, it seems, a Christianized version of the magical cauldrons owned by many Celtic deities, such as the Dagda.

When Welsh and Cornish settlers moved to Brittany, they took stories of Arthur with them. From Brittany, French writers learned of the British hero and began composing romances—long poems—about the adventures of Arthur and the knights and ladies of his court. These Arthurian romances became extremely popular, and soon they were being written in Germany and England as well. Ever since then, tales of King Arthur have remained among the best-loved stories in the world. In the twentieth century there have been numerous books, films, and even a Broadway musical

The legends of King Arthur have fascinated and entertained people since the Middle Ages. In the twentieth century, English author T. H. White wrote a popular novel about Arthur and his court, The Once and Future King. *Alan Jay Lerner and Frederick Loewe used this book as the basis for their Broadway musical* Camelot. *This is a scene from the movie version of* Camelot, *made in 1967.*

retelling the Arthurian legends—and, through those legends, many myths of the ancient Celts.

Celtic Renaissance

It might be said that language is at the heart of a culture. It certainly is one of the strongest forces for cultural identity. The ancient Celtic language had two branches, one spoken in Ireland and the other spoken in Britain and Gaul. Over the course of time, the first branch developed into Irish, Scottish Gaelic, and Manx (the language of the Isle of Man). The second branch became Welsh, Cornish, and Breton (the language of Brittany). All of these languages are highly expressive, with a sensitive, musical quality. For many centuries they thrived in the Celtic lands at the western fringes of Europe.

Then, in the twelfth century, England began a slow conquest of Ireland. By the seventeenth century, English laws and institutions were becoming well established—including the official use of the English language instead of Irish. English domination of Ireland continued to increase, and in 1801 Ireland was officially made part of the British Empire.

The same sort of thing happened in the other Celtic lands, with foreign nations gaining ever greater power and eventually complete political control. In 1532 Brittany became part of France. Wales came under English rule in 1543. Scotland was joined to England in 1707.

These unions posed the most serious threat to the survival of Celtic culture since the Roman and Anglo-Saxon conquests, for the Celtic languages were not recognized by the new rulers. English (in Brittany, French) was the language used by those in power, whether in business or in government. The native languages were suppressed to the point of being practically outlawed—they could not even be taught in school. They began to die.

In the eighteenth century, many people in Wales realized that their culture was in trouble, and they decided to take action. Societies for the preservation of the Welsh language were founded. Old poetic forms were revived. There were even attempts to reconstruct the ancient orders of the bards and druids.

These things were all part of an effort to encourage the Welsh people to think of themselves as a culturally united nation. Nationalist feelings grew steadily in Wales, and the Welsh won many important political rights. Cultural goals were achieved as well, and by the end of the nineteenth century, Wales had its own university, national museum, and national library. At last, in 1942, the Welsh language was given formal, legal recognition by the English government. Today Welsh is not only alive but growing, with everything from road signs to film scripts being written in the Celtic tongue.

In the nineteenth century, Ireland lost roughly a quarter of its population to a series of famines and massive emigration to the United States. For those left on the island, English policies were

Road signs in County Clare today show the two official languages of Ireland: Irish and English.

felt to be ever more oppressive. Irish leaders began to fight for independence from England.

Many in Ireland at this time saw that there was a great need to restore the Irish cultural heritage. At the head of this movement were Lady Augusta Gregory and William Butler Yeats (yates), regarded as one of the world's greatest poets. Lady Gregory translated the tales of Cu Chulainn and the Ulster heroes into English, making them widely available for the first time. Her book was a huge success, and it deeply impressed Yeats, who began to write poems about Cu Chulainn and other figures from ancient Ireland.

Around Yeats gathered a whole group of writers, and together they created the Irish Literary Revival. As part of this, in 1899 Yeats and Lady Gregory founded what was to become the world-famous Abbey Theatre. Plays based on ancient Irish mythology and history as well as plays about Irish peasant life were presented there. Many of the plays were written by the theater's founders, and many of them are still performed today. Lady Gregory, Yeats, and their literary friends ensured that the Irish people would always remember a past that they could be proud of.

An Independent Ireland

Meanwhile work toward Irish independence had been furiously continuing. In 1921 a treaty between the Irish and the English split Ireland in two. Northern Ireland remained under English rule. The rest of the island became the Republic of Ireland. This free Celtic nation has two official languages, Irish and English. Most of the people do not use Irish on a daily basis, but all children learn it in school. There are major poets and authors who write in Irish, and many singers who perform and record songs in Irish.

In the other Celtic lands today the languages are hanging on with varying strength. Manx is little used, although the Isle of Man is almost completely independent of England. The portion of the Scottish population that speaks Gaelic is steadily decreasing. On the other hand, there is a movement toward Scottish independence and much interest in cultural heritage, including traditional music and Gaelic songs, so the language may still be rescued from extinction. In Brittany there is a great deal of nationalist feeling, and this has centered on reviving and strengthening the Breton language.

And in Cornwall something almost miraculous is happening: The Cornish language, which ceased to be spoken at all in the eighteenth century, is being brought back to life. Celtic languages are being learned elsewhere, too, particularly in the United States and Canada, which have received large numbers of immigrants from the Celtic lands.

The Celts of today live very differently from their ancestors. But although much of the ancient culture is dead, much of what was best in it is thriving: the love of music, poetry, storytelling, and imagination; the love of beauty; and the love of freedom.

The ancient Celts left no great buildings or monuments, but they nevertheless left a lasting impression on the lands they inhabited. Folktales that can still be heard today tell how the hero Fionn MacCumhaill built the Giant's Causeway, a natural rock formation in Northern Ireland. In this and many other ways the spirit of the Celts lives on.

The Ancient Celts: A Chronology

B.C.E.

c. 700	Hallstatt era of Celtic culture begins
c. 600	Hallstatt culture reaches Ireland
c. 450	La Tène era of Celtic culture begins
c. 400	Celtic tribes invade northern Italy
390	Celts defeat Romans at Clusium, then attack Rome
285	Romans exterminate the Celtic tribe of the Senones
279	Celts attack Greek city of Delphi
278	Celts enter Asia Minor
275	Founding of Celtic kingdom of Galatia in Asia Minor; Celtic territory at its greatest extent
225	Romans defeat Celts at Telamon
225–190	Romans drive Celts out of northern Italy
124	Romans defeat Celts in southern Gaul
120	Roman province established in southern Gaul
59	Celtic tribe of the Helvetii begins westward migration
58	Julius Caesar defeats the Helvetii
58–56	Caesar conquers Gaul
55 and 54	Caesar makes two expeditions to Britain
53	Rebellion of Ambiorix
52	Rebellion of Vercingetorix
50	Caesar returns to Rome

C.E.

43	Roman invasion of Britain
47	Roman army advances into Wales and Cornwall
51	Cartimandua allies herself with the Romans
c. 60	Romans attack the druids of Anglesey; rebellion of Boudicca
71–84	Roman conquest of northern Britain and southern Scotland
410	Roman Empire abandons Britain
c. 450	Christianity spreads through Ireland

GLOSSARY

archaeologist: a person who studies the remains, such as tools and weapons, of past human cultures

artisan: a person skilled in a particular craft, for example, a metalworker, jeweler, or carver

bard: a Celtic poet of Britain or Gaul

bronze: a metal alloy composed mainly of copper and tin

carnyx: a trumpet whose bell was usually shaped like an animal head

client: a freeman who provided food, manual labor, hospitality, and military service to a more influential freeman in return for various kinds of assistance

concubine: a legally recognized mistress

divination: the art of foretelling the future or discovering hidden knowledge

fian (FYEE-uhn): an elite Irish war band, which could include women as well as men

fidchell (FYIH-hehl): "wood wisdom"; a popular Celtic board game, somewhat like chess; called *gwyddbwyll* (GOO-ihth-boo-ihth) in Wales

fili (FYIH-lyih): a highly educated Irish poet who also practiced the arts of divination and prophecy

fosterage: the practice of sending one's children to be raised and educated by someone higher on the social scale

genealogy: story of the descent of an individual, family, or group from an ancestor

grianan (GREE-uh-nawn): "sunroom"; a balcony or upper-story room that overlooked the first floor of a wealthy Irish house, usually reserved for women

guerilla warfare: a style of warfare that relies on ambushes and hit-and-run techniques rather than on open battle

illumination: an illustration in a medieval manuscript

lintel: architectural strip above a window or door that supports the opening

monasticism: groups of religious women or men living in communities devoted to prayer and study

mythology: a group of tales passed on through generations that deal with gods, demigods, or legendary heroes

oppidum (OH-pee-dum): a fortified village

pastoralism: a lifestyle that centers on raising herds of animals

personify: to give human or lifelike qualities to a thing or idea

reincarnation: the rebirth of the soul into a new body after death

ritual: a religious ceremony

ritually: done in a formal way according to religious tradition

romance: a medieval story or long poem that usually combines knightly love and adventure with elements of legend and the supernatural

sacred: holy

scabbard: a case for the blade of a sword or dagger, often decorated; sheath

torc: a thick neck ring of twisted metal worn by Celtic nobles and warriors

triskele (TRY-skeel): a design with three branches moving in the same direction around a central point, frequently used in Celtic art

tunic: a simple slip-on garment made with or without sleeves. Usually worn knee-length or longer, it was often belted at the waist.

FOR FURTHER READING

*Gantz, Jeffrey, trans. *Early Irish Myths and Sagas.* Harmondsworth: Penguin, 1981.

Hodges, Henry, and Edward Pyddoke. *Ancient Britons: How They Lived.* New York: Praeger, 1969.

Hodges, Margaret. *The Other World: Myths of the Celts.* New York: Farrar, Straus and Giroux, 1973.

*Jackson, Kenneth Hurlstone, trans. *A Celtic Miscellany.* Harmondsworth: Penguin, 1971.

Martell, Hazel Mary. *What Do We Know about the Celts?* New York: Peter Bedrick, 1993.

Pittenger, W. Norman. *Early Britain: The Celtics, Romans, and Anglo-Saxons.* New York: Franklin Watts, 1972.

Place, Robin. *The Celts.* London: Macdonald; Morristown, New Jersey: Silver Burdett, 1977.

Ross, Anne. *Druids, Gods, and Heroes from Celtic Mythology.* New York: Schocken Books; Vancouver: Douglas and McIntyre, 1986.

*Williamson, Robin. *The Wise and Foolish Tongue: Celtic Stories and Poems.* San Francisco: Chronicle Books, 1991.

*Although these books are intended for adults, they contain much to interest young readers.

BIBLIOGRAPHY

Bromwich, Rachel, ed. and trans. *Trioedd Ynys Prydein: The Welsh Triads.* 2d ed. Cardiff: University of Wales Press, 1978.

Chadwick, Nora. *The Celts.* Harmondsworth: Penguin, 1970.

Cunliffe, Barry. *The Celtic World.* New York: McGraw-Hill, 1979.

Ford, Patrick, trans. *The Mabinogion.* Berkeley: University of California Press, 1977.

Gantz, Jeffrey, trans. *Early Irish Myths and Sagas.* Harmondsworth: Penguin, 1981.

Gray, Elizabeth, ed. and trans. *Cath Maige Tuired.* Kildare: Irish Texts Society, 1982.

Herm, Gerhard. *The Celts: The People Who Came Out of the Darkness.* New York: St. Martin's, 1976.

Hutton, Ronald. *The Pagan Religions of the Ancient British Isles.* Cambridge, Massachusetts, and Oxford: Blackwell, 1991.

Kinsella, Thomas, trans. *The Tain.* London: Oxford University Press, 1969.

Logan, Patrick. *The Old Gods: The Facts about the Irish Fairies.* Belfast: Appletree, 1981.

Loomis, Roger Sherman. *The Development of Arthurian Romance.* New York: Harper & Row, 1963.

Markale, Jean. *The Celts: Uncovering the Mythic and Historic Origins of Western Culture.* Rochester, Vermont: Inner Traditions, 1993.

Markale, Jean. *Women of the Celts.* Rochester, Vermont: Inner Traditions, 1986.

Rees, Alwyn, and Brinley Rees. *Celtic Heritage: Ancient Tradition in Ireland and Wales.* New York: Thames and Hudson, 1961; rpt. 1990.

Ross, Anne. *Everyday Life of the Pagan Celts.* London: B. T. Batsford; New York: G. P. Putnam's Sons, 1970.

Ross, Anne. *Pagan Celtic Britain: Studies in Iconography and Tradition.* New York: Columbia University Press; London: Routledge and Kegan Paul, 1967.

Sjoestedt, Marie-Louise. *Gods and Heroes of the Celts.* Trans. Myles Dillon. Berkeley, California: Turtle Island Foundation, 1982.

Squire, Charles. *Celtic Myth and Legend, Poetry and Romance.* Van Nuys, California: Newcastle, 1975.

INDEX

Page numbers for illustrations are in boldface

ABOUT THE AUTHOR

Kathryn Hinds has been fascinated by Celtic literature and mythology for most of her life. She grew up near Rochester, New York, then moved to New York City to study music and writing at Barnard College. She did graduate work in comparative literature at the City University of New York, where she took a course in Old Irish. For several years she has worked as a freelance editor of children's books. She also writes poetry, which has been published in a number of magazines. Ms. Hinds now lives in the north Georgia mountains with her husband, their son, and two cats. Her other books in this series are *The Ancient Romans* and *India's Gupta Dynasty*.